The neat houses of Quality Street in Merstham (Stage 3)

THE NORTH DOWNS WAY

The North Downs Way is a 130 mile (208km) route between Farnham and Dover through the Surrey and Kent AONBs. It traces a high chalk ridge of downland with views over the Weald and the 'garden of England'.

Contents and using this guide

This booklet of Ordnance Survey 1:25,000 Explorer maps has been designed for convenient use on the trail and includes:

- a key to map pages (page 2–3) showing where to find the maps for each stage.
- the full and up-to-date line of the National Trail
- an extract from the OS Explorer map legend (pages 85–87).

In addition, the *North Downs Way* guidebook describes the full route from west to east and contains all you need to plan a successful trip.

© Cicerone Press 2017
ISBN: 978 1 85284 955 9
Photos © Kev Reynolds 2017

Map data

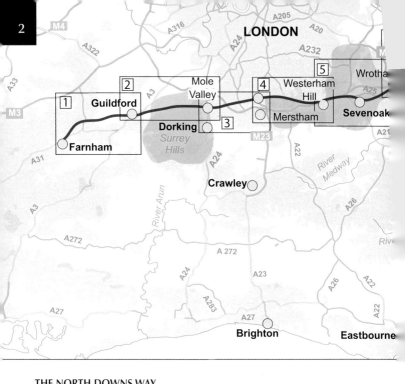

THE NORTH DOWNS WAY

DIRECT ROUTE TO DOVER VIA WYE

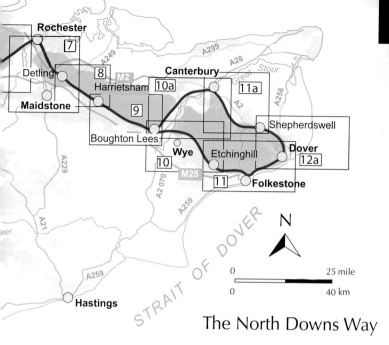

The North Downs Way

THE CANTERBURY LOOP

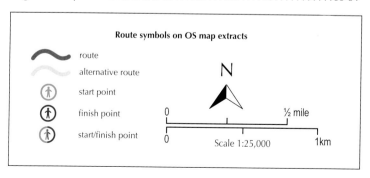

Route symbols on OS map extracts

route

alternative route

start point

finish point

start/finish point

N

0   ½ mile

0   1km

Scale 1:25,000

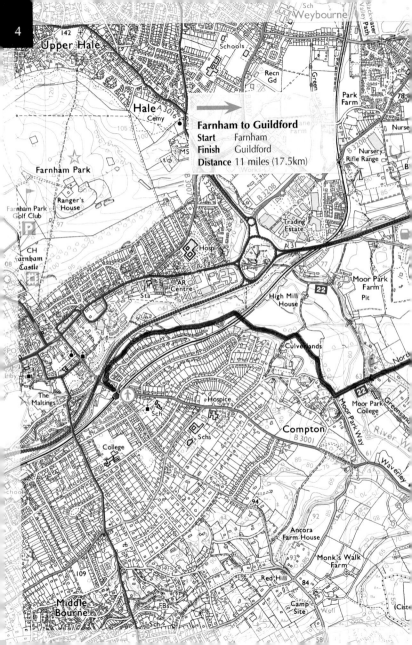

Farnham to Guildford

Start	Farnham
Finish	Guildford
Distance	11 miles (17.5km)

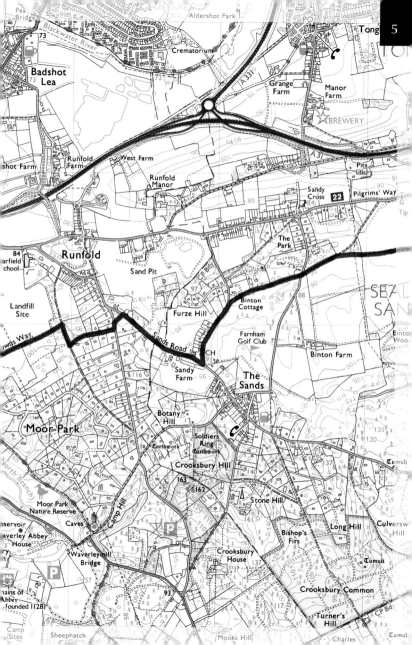

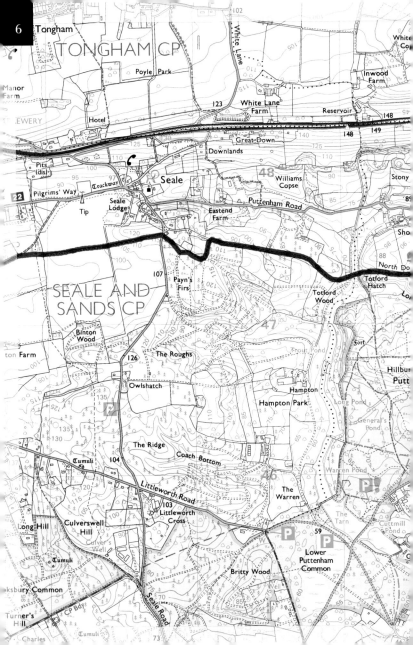

Wanborough Wood

Wanborough

Wanborough Manor

Manor
Farm

Pit
(dis)

grass
se

Hog's Back

A31

Quarry
(dis)

Puttenham
Hill

P

Sch

Puttenham

Priory

Clear
Barn

Seale Lane

104

Cumulus

22

Little Common

Cemy

Puttenham H

CH

B 3000

Little
Lascombe

Suffield
Farm

's Way

Fox Way

Hook Lane

Hurlands

Lascombe
Farm

Pit
(dis)

92

Bottom

Gore's
Farm

89

98

PUTTENHAM CP

ham Common

Church Croft

108

Lone Barn

P

Lydling
Farm

SHACKLEFORD CP

73

Chalk Lane

Rodsall
Manor

Cross
Farm

Shackleford

Sch

PO

Roker's Lane (Path)

Mill
Marsh

The
Marsh

Mitchen Hall
Plantation

Redhill
Plantation

74

Ho
Far

Broad Firs

Mitchen
Hall

Gatwick

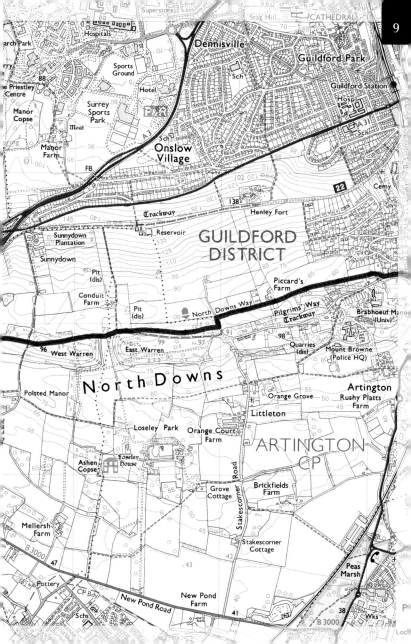

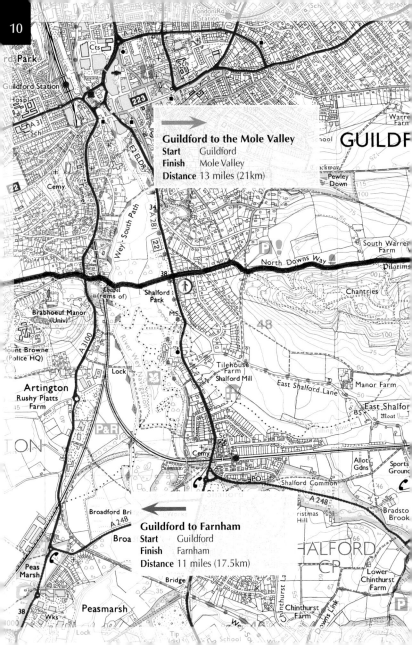

Guildford to the Mole Valley

Start   Guildford
Finish   Mole Valley
Distance 13 miles (21km)

Guildford to Farnham

Start   Guildford
Finish   Farnham
Distance 11 miles (17.5km)

CH
Guildford Golf Club
Trodd's Lane
Merrow Downs
Walnut Tree Bottom
Urn Field
Harewarren
The Roughs
Burwood Farm
BS
ORD
Reservoir
Trackway
BS
P
i
Ne
Albu
White Lane Farm
Tyting Farm
Tumulus
Keepers Cottage
Pilgrims' Way
Guildford Lane
hinny Way
Halfpenny La
St Martha's Hill
P
BS
Colyers Hanger
Albury Mill
Resr
Great Halfpenny Farm
Downs Link
Longfrey Farm
Marigold Cottage
BS
BS
Fish Ponds
Chilworth Manor
Little Wa
52
Wate
Postford Ponds
Postford House
Cuckoo Copse
Little Halfpenny Farm
ST MARTHA CP
Tilling Bourne
Lockner Farm
Mud Wood
Chilworth
Sch
War Mem
Lockner Lodge
Water Tower
94
Watercress B (disused)
PO
Chilworth Station
Lockner Holt
Postfo Cott
48
School
CP Bdy
Brooks Wood
Tangley Mere
Great Tangley Manor House
Hornhatch Farm
Moat
Great Tangley Manor Farm
Tangley Hill
Monastery
Rosemary Hill
War Mem
Blackheath
Wonersh Common
Little Tangley
Blackheath
P
Blackheath

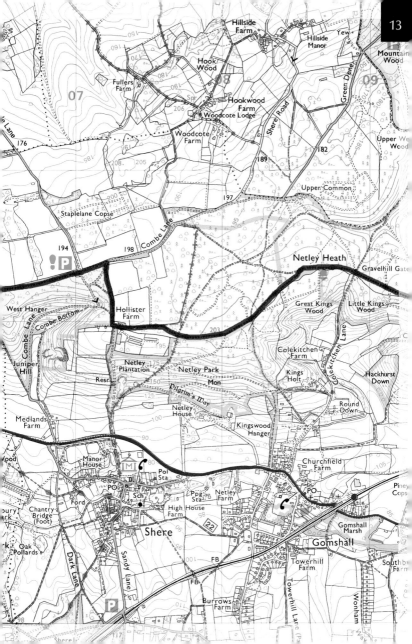

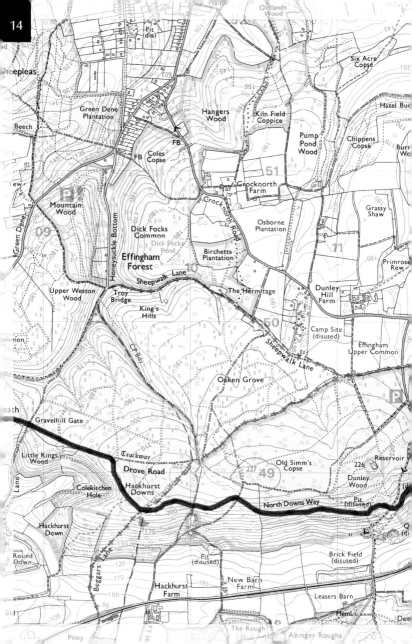

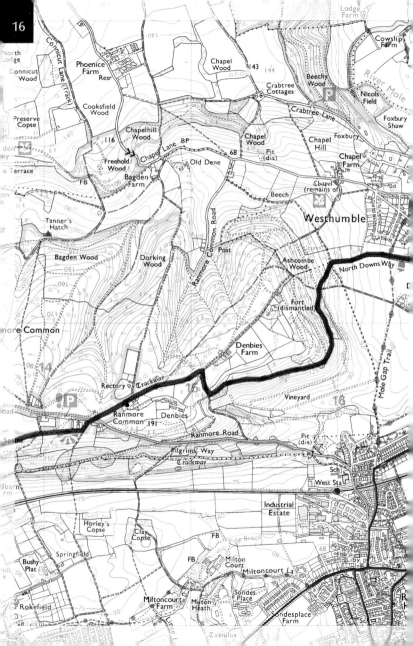

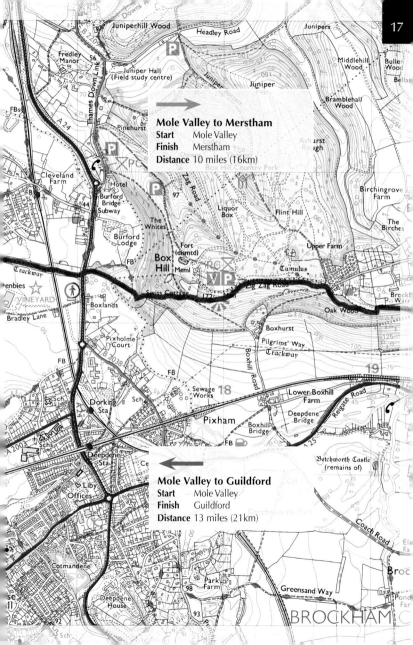

Mole Valley to Merstham
Start   Mole Valley
Finish   Merstham
Distance 10 miles (16km)

Mole Valley to Guildford
Start   Mole Valley
Finish   Guildford
Distance 13 miles (21km)

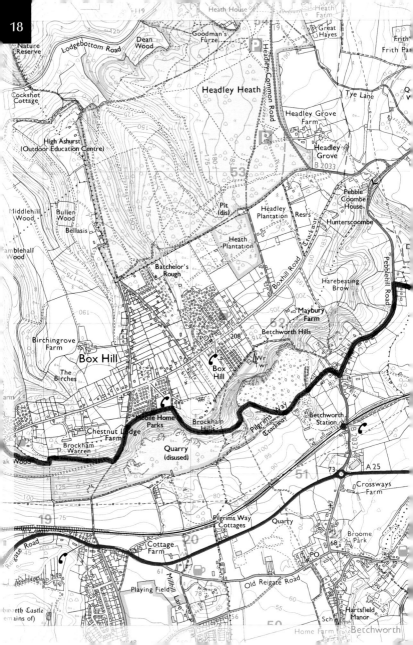

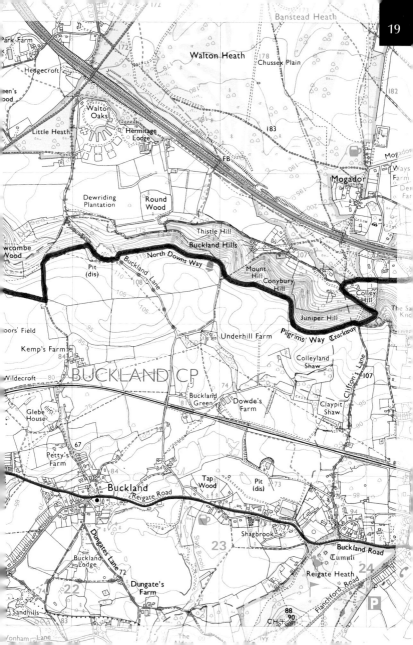

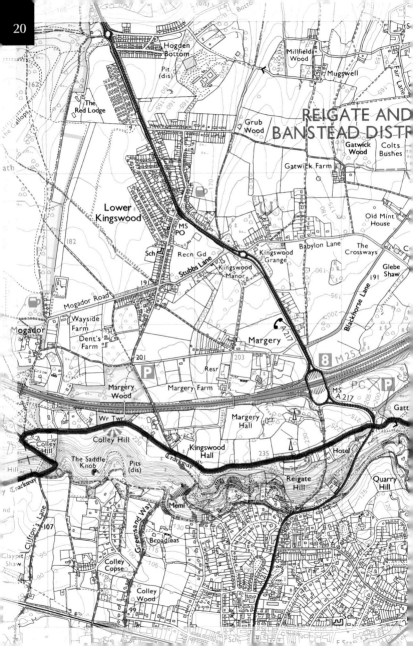

Hogden
Bottom

Pit
(dis)

Millfield
Wood

Mugswell

The
Red Lodge

the Gallops

ath

Grub
Wood

REIGATE AND
BANSTEAD DISTR

Gatwick
Wood

Colts
Bushes

Gatwick Farm

Lower
Kingswood

MS
PO

Sch

Recn Gd

Stubbs Lane

Kingswood
Manor

Kingswood
Grange

Babylon Lane

Old Mint
House

The
Crossways

Glebe
Shaw

191

Blackhorse Lane

Mogador Road

191

Wayside
Farm

Mogador

Dent's
Farm

201

Margery

A 217

203

8 M25

Margery
Wood

P

Resr

Margery Farm

MS
A 217

PC

P

Gatt

Wr Twr

Colley Hill

Margery
Hall

Margery
Hall

Hotel

Colley
Hill

The Saddle
Knob

Pits
(dis)

Kingswood
Hall

Crackmar

235

Reigate
Hill

Quarry
Hill

Hill

Trackway

Clifton's Lane

Greensand Way

Mem

Broadleas

130

Claypit
Shaw

107

Colley
Copse

Colley
Wood

99

Sch

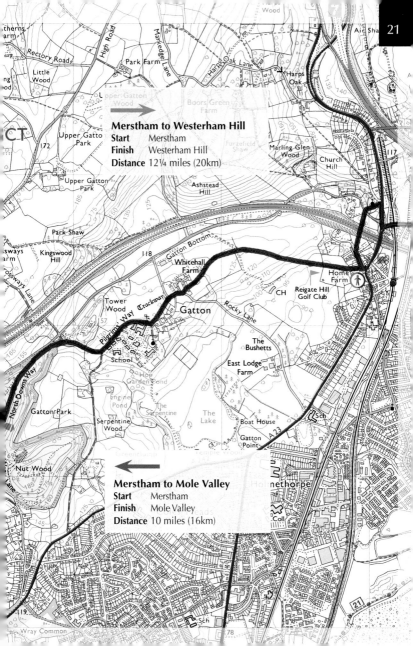

Merstham to Westerham Hill
Start Merstham
Finish Westerham Hill
Distance 12¼ miles (20km)

Merstham to Mole Valley
Start Merstham
Finish Mole Valley
Distance 10 miles (16km)

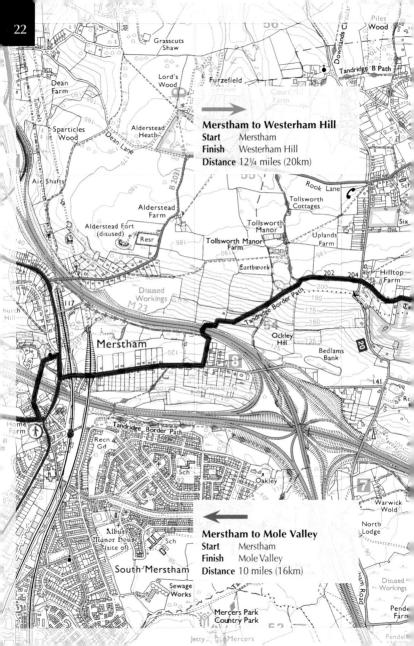

Merstham to Westerham Hill
Start Merstham
Finish Westerham Hill
Distance 12¼ miles (20km)

Merstham to Mole Valley
Start Merstham
Finish Mole Valley
Distance 10 miles (16km)

Broad
Wood

CH

Fryern Broom
Wood

Surrey National
Golf Club

Fryern
Farm

Sch

CATERHAM

Sch

Queen's Park

Hospl

Cemy

Liby

B2030

Chaldon

Rook
Farm

CHALDON CP

others
ld

194

Roffes Lane

Beech
Hanger

Sch

Sch

148

Sch

WT Sta

Downlands Circular Walk

North Downs Way

Pilgrims' Lane

Upton
Farm

Sch

Willey Park
Farm

White
Hill

Quarry Hangers

Arthur's Seat

Tower
Farm

Weald Way

CATERHAM
VALLEY
CP

Oldpark
Wood

Spring Bottom Lane

Quarry
Cottages

haw
se

Track way

203

Wr
Twr

Gravelly
Hill

Quarry Hall
Farm

Pendell
Wood

154

Fort

White Rose
Farm

War Coppice
House

Black
Bushes

21

Whitehill
Roughts

Black
Bushes

Kitchen
Copse

Green Lane (Track)

Big Pickle

North Park
Farm

Water Lane (Track)

109

Place Farm

Becks
Cottage

Orchard
Cottage

Elm Platt

Brewerstreet

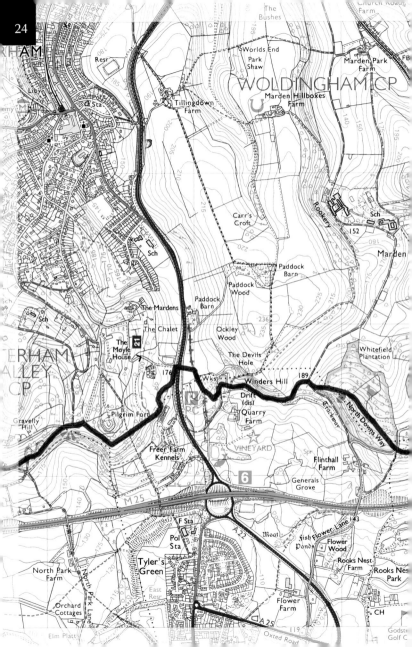

Woldingham

Valleyfields

Greenhill Shaw

Little Church Wood

Whistlers Wood Farm

Southview Road

Vanguard Way

Wr Twr
WT Sta

Whistlers Wood

Enclosure

Flint House

Woldingham Road

CH

Southfields Road

Northdown Road

North Downs Golf Club

Great Church Wood

Trackway

P

252

Beech Plantation

Air Shafts

Tunnel

248

Quarry Works

Greensand Way

Stubbs Copse

P

South Hawke

BPs

Pilgrims' Way

Trackway

Spr

Chalkpit Wood

Gangers Hill

Lodge Wood

Five Acre Shaw

Tandridge Hill

Schs

Haldons Farm

120

Hanging Wood

Tandridgehill Farm

Robins Grove Wood

Barrow Green Court

110

Barrow Green Farm

Blunt House

Cemy

The Abbeys

103

The-Bogs

North Model Farm

Sandy Lane

Oxted

Palmer's Wood

Weirs

The Mount

Townland Pond

103

Barrow Green Road

Priory Shaw

105

Disused Workings

The Priory

108

Tandridgehill Lane

160

135

115

MS

A25

Mill

Ashen
Shaw
Shaw

Kitchen
Grove
Enclosures

ROMAN ROAD
(course of)

PO
229
Sch

Croydon Road

Cheverells
Farm

Beaver
Water World

Beacon Shaw
Waylands

Approach Road

Beddlestead Lane

Pitchers Wood

56
262

Clarks
Farm

TITSEY CP

Paygate
Cottage

B 269

Trackway

258
High Trees

White Lane

Titsey Hill

Pilgrims Fa

Botley Hill
Farm

Botley Hill

North Downs Way

267

WT Sta

P

Pitchfont Lane

55

Evelyn
Avenue

171

Titsey Place

Twr

139

Titsey
Park

139
Titsey

Wr
Sta

Enclosure

Woldingham Road

Titsey
Plantation

126

Flint
House

Pitchfont
Farm

ROMAN VILLA
(remains of)

Greensand
Way

Vanguard Way

FB
108

Titsey Road

River Eden

Chalkpit
Wood

Ford
Limpsfield
Grange
Sch

101

Hookwood
163

Schs

Cemy
Schs

B 269

FB

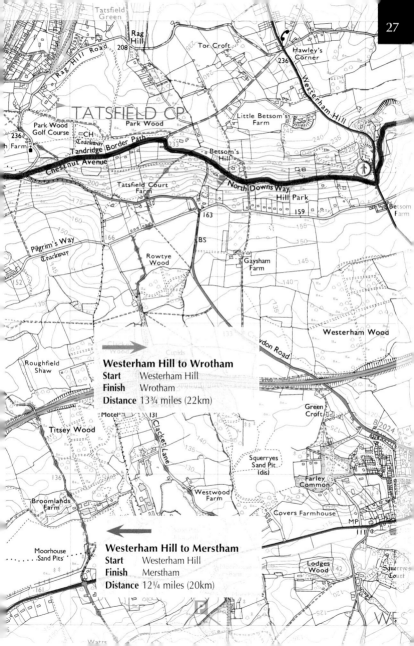

Westerham Hill to Wrotham
Start   Westerham Hill
Finish   Wrotham
Distance 13¾ miles (22km)

Westerham Hill to Merstham
Start   Westerham Hill
Finish   Merstham
Distance 12¼ miles (20km)

Westerham Hill to Wrotham

Start	Westerham Hill
Finish	Wrotham
Distance	13¾ miles (22km)

Westerham Hill to Merstham

Start	Westerham Hill
Finish	Merstham
Distance	12¼ miles (20km)

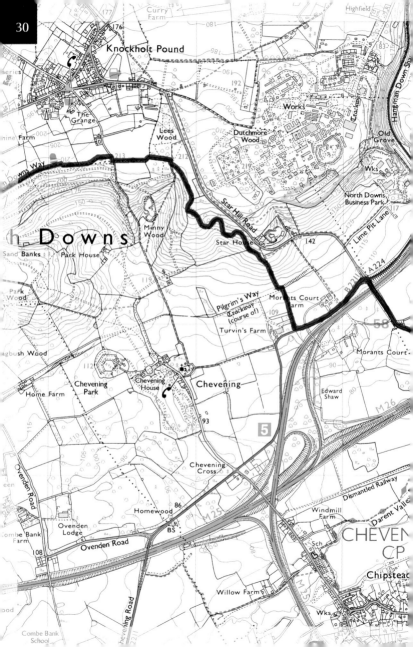

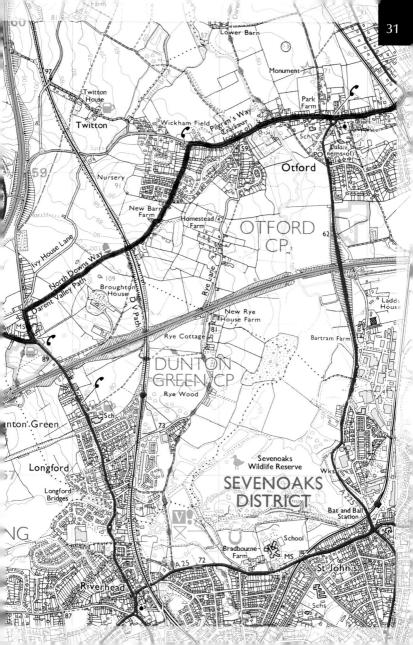

Magpie
Bottom

Whitehill
Farm

Doctor's
Wood

Rose Cottage
Farm

Littlehurst
Farm

Warren
Farm

187

Eastdown

Stevenacre
Stubs

Highfield

Fackenden Down
Nature Reserve

Trackway

53

54

55

Paine's
Farm

Great Wood

Birchin Cross Road

Tel Ex

Greenhill
Wood

Mount Fm

91

204

Resr

Shorehill Farm

Hillydeal
Wood

North Downs Way

Otford Mount

Tumulus

School

Rowdow
Wood

208

Shore Hill

Otford Manc

Kemsing Down
Nature Reserve

Palace
(remsof)

ROMAN
VILLA

104

Pilgrim's Way
Trackway

PO

102

Oxenhill
Shaw

Kemsing

Dynes Farm

Ladds
House

Childsbridge
House

Childsbridge

Noah's Ark

Clay Pit

Penfield

Bluebell
Farm

Sand Pit

Greatness

Sch

Church St

Cemy

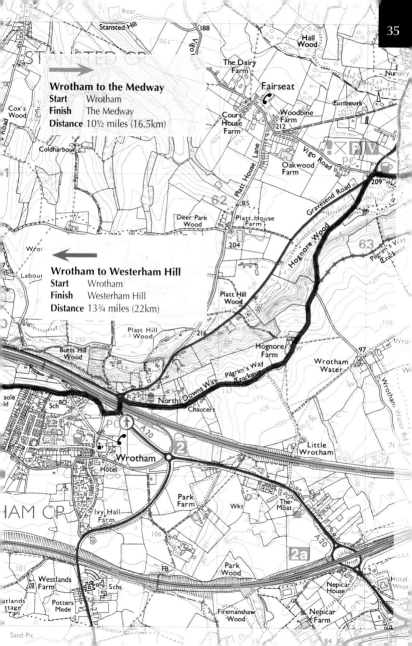

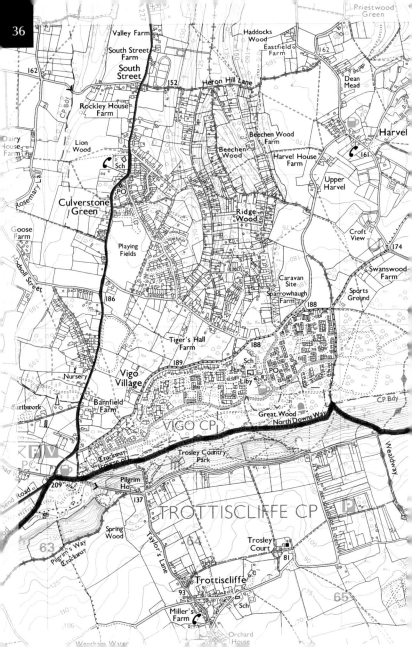

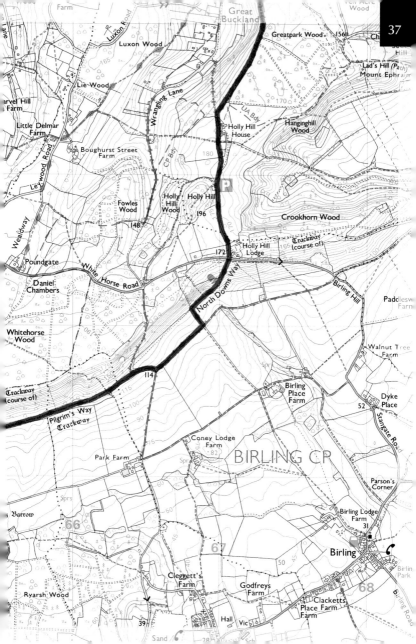

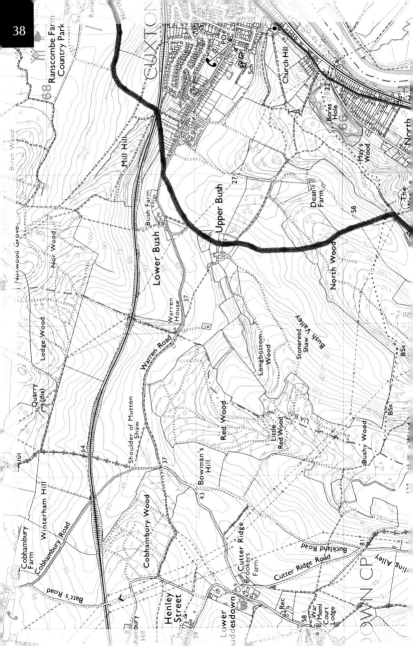

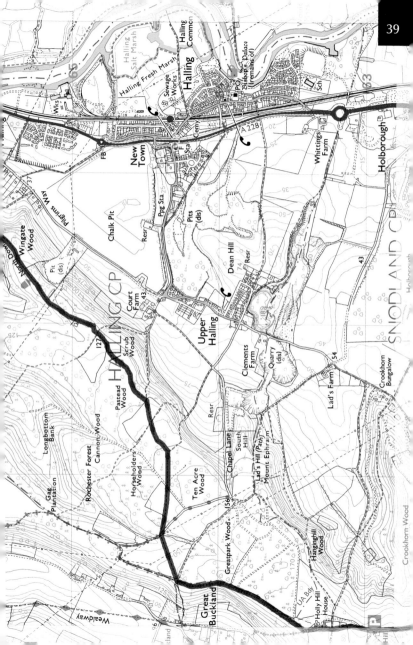

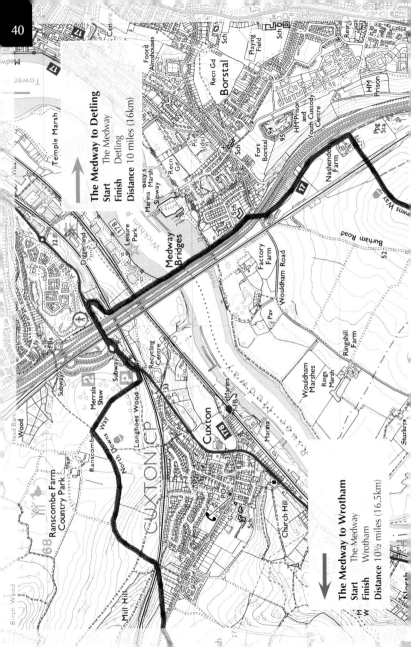

The Medway to Detling

Start The Medway
Finish Detling
Distance 10 miles (16km)

The Medway to Wrotham

Start The Medway
Finish Wrotham
Distance 10½ miles (16.5km)

Borstal

HM Prison

Temple Marsh

Medway Bridges

Cuxton

CUXTON CP

Ranscombe Farm Country Park

Mill Hill

Birch Wood

Head Barn Wood

Merrals Shaw

Longhoes Wood

North Downs Way

Ranscombe Way

Subway

Recycling Centre

Wickham R

Leisure Park

Digterland

Factory Farm

Wouldham Road

Burham Road

Nashenden Farm

Fort Borstal

HM Prison and Youth Custody Centre

Foord Almshouses

Playing Field

Recn Gd

Wouldham Marshes

Rings Marsh

Ringshill Farm

Marina

Church Hill

Marina Marsh Slipway

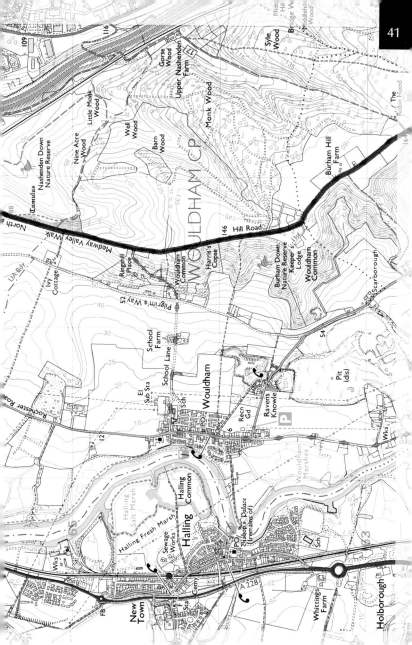

Syle Wood

Bridge Wood

Gorse Wood

Upper Nashenden Farm

Little Monk Wood

Monk Wood

Well Wood

Nashenden Down Nature Reserve

Nine Acre Wood

Barn Wood

The Robin Hood

Burham Hill Farm

WOULDHAM CP

North Downs

Medway Valley Walk

Tumulus

Hill Road

146

145

Burham Down Nature Reserve

Keeper's Lodge

Wouldham Common

Ringshill Place

Harris's Copse

Wouldham Common

(V) Cottage

UA Bdy

Scarborough

Pilgrim's Way

52

40

30

School Farm

School Lane

Rochester Road

El Sub Sta

Sch

Wouldham

PO

Recn Gd

Ravens Knowle

Pit (dis)

P

Wks

Wouldham Marshes

Halling Salt Marsh

Halling Common

Halling Fresh Marsh

Halling

Bishop's Palace (remains of)

PO

Sch

Wks

Sewage Works

Cem

FB

New Town

A 228

Whitings Farm

Holborough

Taddington
Wood

The Robin Hood

Buckmore
Park

Lord
Lees

164

Burham Common

3

Common Road

A 229

FB

North Downs Way

Blue Bell
Hill

BURHAM CP

Meml

Impton
Wood

Hall

Pits
(dis)

P

Crematorium

Subwa

Sch

42

Kit's Coty

ROMAN ROAD

Frith Wood

Tunnel

Kit's Coty
Farm

Petts
Farm

Pit
(dis)

194

Little
Culand

North

Dow

Hale Farm

17

FB

Sch
36

Kit's Coty House
Burial Chamber

MS

Lower W

59

50

North

75

War
Meml

74

Moat

Sprs

Little Kit's
Coty House
Burial Chamber

Downs Way

White
Horse
Stone

Eccles

40

45

Subway

Wellhead

AYLESFORD CP

25

20

Cowleaze
Farm

24

62

A 229

ROMAN ROAD

Sand Pit

Anchor Farm

Rochester Road

Little
Cossington
Farm

21

Great
Cossington

4

Aylesford

Pratling
Street

CP Bdy

FB

Tylan

CH

Court
Farm

Sch

Industrial Estate

Sports
Ground

Forstal

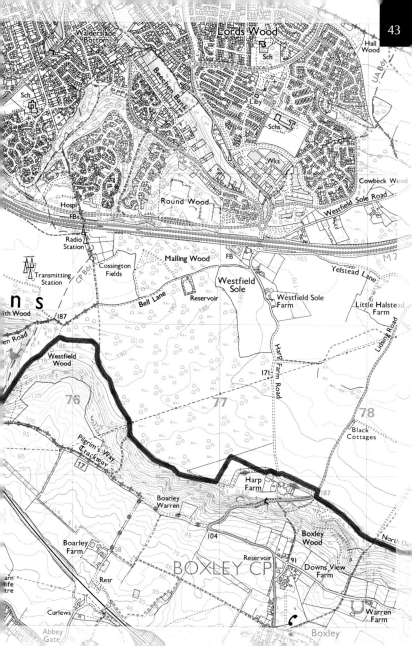

Detling to Harrietsham
Start   Detling
Finish   Harrietsham
Distance 7½ miles (12km)

Detling to the Medway
Start   Detling
Finish   The Medway
Distance 10 miles (16km)

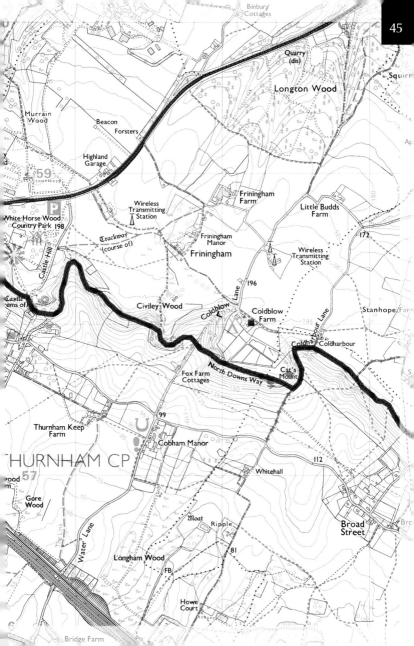

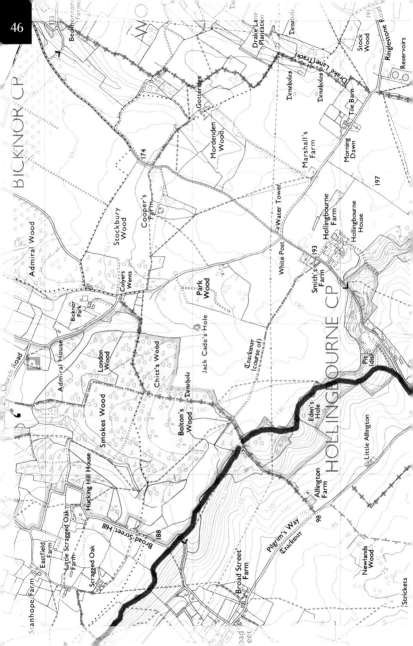

BICKNOR CP

Beamonton

WOOD

Drake Lane Plantation

Denehole

Stock Wood

Ringlestone Road

Reservoirs

Drake Lane (Track)

Deneholes

Deneholes

Tile Barn

Gotteridge

Mordenden Wood

Marshall's Farm

Morning Dawn

197

174

Water Tower

Cooper's Farm

Stockbury Wood

White Post

193

Smith's Farm

Hollingbourne Farm

Hollingbourne House

Admiral Wood

190

Colyers Wents

Park Wood

HOLLINGBOURNE CP

Bicknor Park

Church Road

Admiral House

London Wood

Chitt's Wood

Jack Cade's Hole

Trackway (course of)

Pil(dis)

Eden's Hole

Little Allington

Smokes Wood

Denehole

Bolton's Wood

190

190

Hucking Hill House

Eastfield Farm

Little Scragged Oak Farm

Broad Street Hill

188

Allington Farm

98

Pilgrim's Way Trackway

95

Newlands Wood

Stanhope Farm

Scragged Oak

Broad Street Farm

Strickets

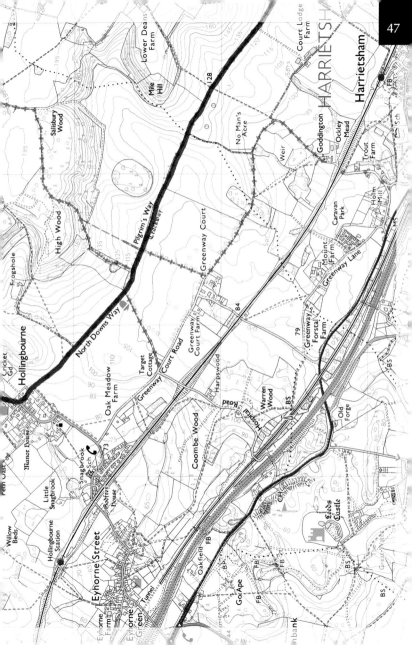

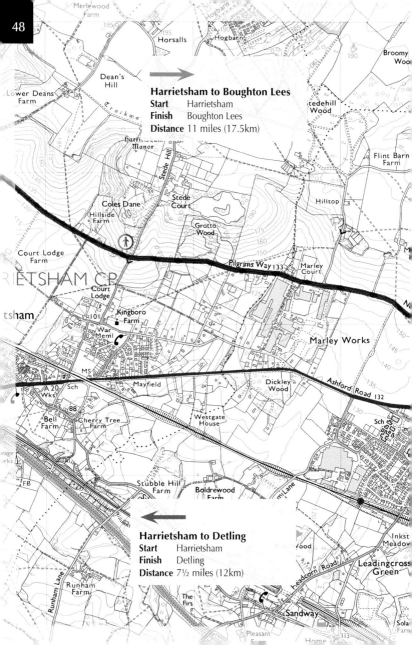

Harrietsham to Boughton Lees
Start   Harrietsham
Finish Boughton Lees
Distance 11 miles (17.5km)

Harrietsham to Detling
Start   Harrietsham
Finish Detling
Distance 7½ miles (12km)

Wood

166

55

Lone Barn Farm

Maitlands Farm

160 155 150

ees

Greenways

Faversham Road

West Street Farm

Forge Cottage

Payden Street Farm

Newage Farm

West Street

47

Lone Barn Road

Payden Street

179

Flint Lane

Trackway

179

Woodside Green

54

192

low rm

Lea Farm

Tophill Farm

Birch Wood

Deneholes

Highfield

Downs Way

53

War Meml

Trackway (course of)

Little Pivington Farm

Middleton Farm

Hubbards Hill 193

Pilgrim's Way

Great Pivington Farm

Trackway

Cemy

PO

109

52

Lenham

F Sta

FB

Tanyard Farm

East Lenham

A 20

Scour Valley Walk

New Shelve Farm

d arm

LENHAM CP

Oxley Wood

Scour Valley Walk

Pipe Line

Wheatgratten Farm

Sewage

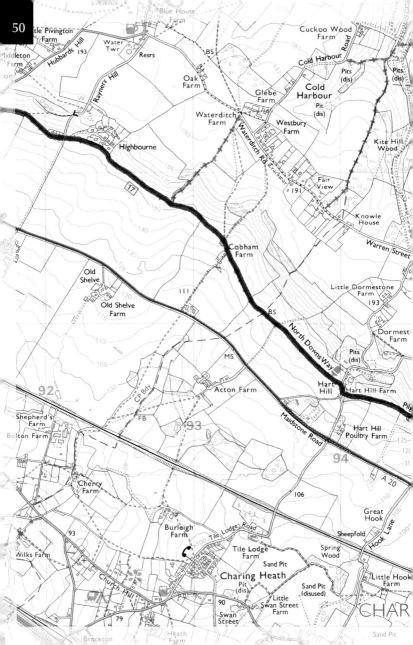

Green Farm
Haylocks Cottages
Norton Hall
158
Hillside Road
111
Stalisfield Green
Rigshill Farm
Rigshill Road
Spuckles Wood
Court Lodge Farm
Kingsbourne Farm
Parsonage Farm
CP Bdy
Pits (dis)
Bank Wood
Cornhill Farm
Arkett's Farm
Vent House
Hurst Wood
onestile
Kenyon Farm
Stalisfield Road
Mill Mound
Bowl Farm
Hawk's Nest
Bottle Farm
Wilderness Farm
Ranpura Farm
Crows Hole Farm
Impkins Farm
Cole Wood
Bowl Road
Trackway
96
Woodville Farm
97
Kenfield Farm
192
Stocker's Head
95
Quarries (dis)
Charing Hill
Resr
Poultry Farm
Gallops
's Way
138
Hotel
101
A 252
Pilgrims Way Trackway
Charing
Lone Barn Farm
Spr
Sch
Palace Farm
Archbishop's Palace (remains of)
Liby PO
Pett Lane
99
Toll Lane
Dencher Wood
17
IG CP
FB
104
Pett Place
Chapel (rems of)
Burnt House Farm
Works
Chalk Pit
Broadway
Alder Bed
Pett Farm

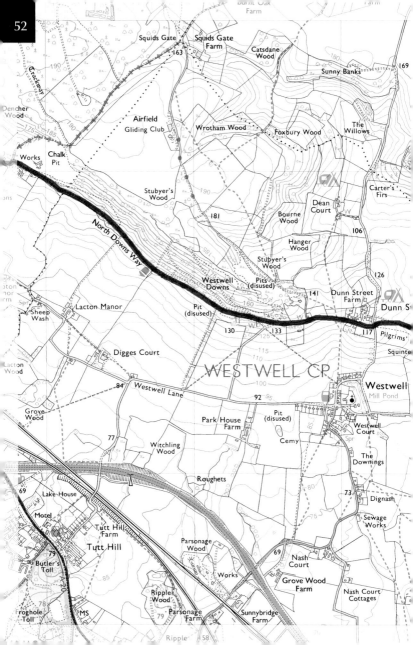

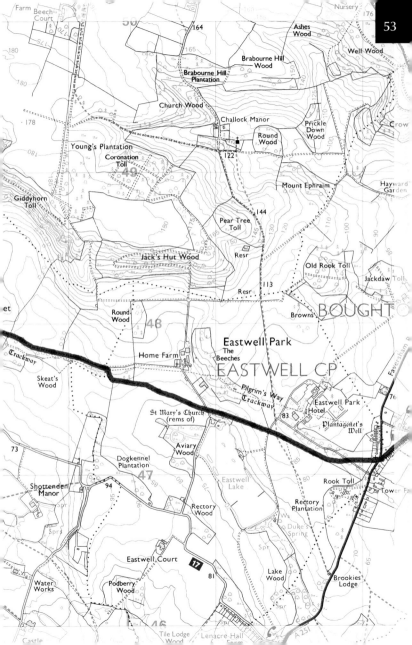

Boughton Lees to Harrietsham
Start   Boughton Lees
Finish   Harrietsham
Distance 11 miles (17.5km)

Boughton Lees to Etchinghill
Start   Boughton Lees
Finish   Etchinghill
Distance 13 miles (21km)

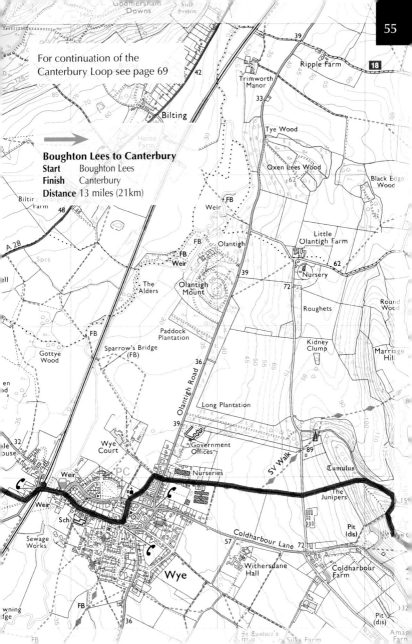

For continuation of the
Canterbury Loop see page 69

Boughton Lees to Canterbury
Start Boughton Lees
Finish Canterbury
Distance 13 miles (21km)

Goodnesham
Downs

Field System

39

Ripple Farm

18

42

Trimworth
Manor

Bilting

33

Tye Wood

Home
Farm

Oxen Lees Wood

Black Edge
Wood

Biltir
Farm

48

Little
Olantigh Farm

FB

Weir

A 28

Sprs

FB

FB
Weir

Olantigh

39

Nursery

62

ll

The
Alders

Olantigh
Mount

72

Roughets

Round
Wood

FB

Paddock
Plantation

Kidney
Clump

Marriage
Hill

Gottye
Wood

Sparrow's Bridge
(FB)

36

Olantigh Road

Long Plantation

45

50

55

65

en
od

35

39

Wye
Court

Government
Offices

SV Walk

89

Tumulus

32

house

Weir

PC

Nurseries

The
Junipers

Weir

Sch

Coldharbour Lane

Pit
(dis)

Sewage
Works

57

72

Wye

Withersdane
Hall

Coldharbour
Farm

FB

36

Pit
(dis)

wning
dge

St Eustace's

Silks Farm

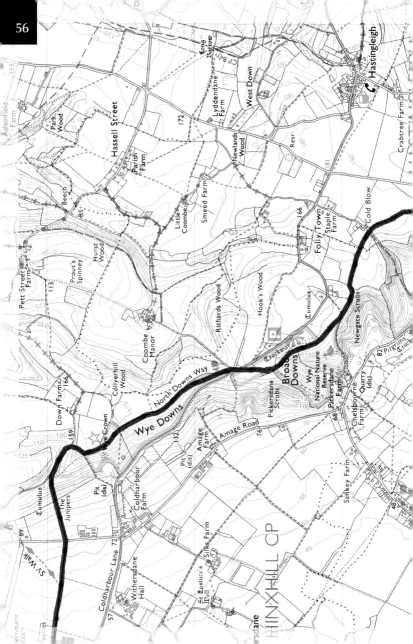

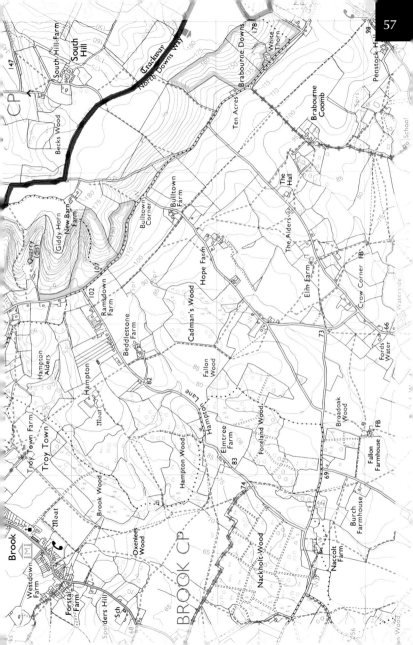

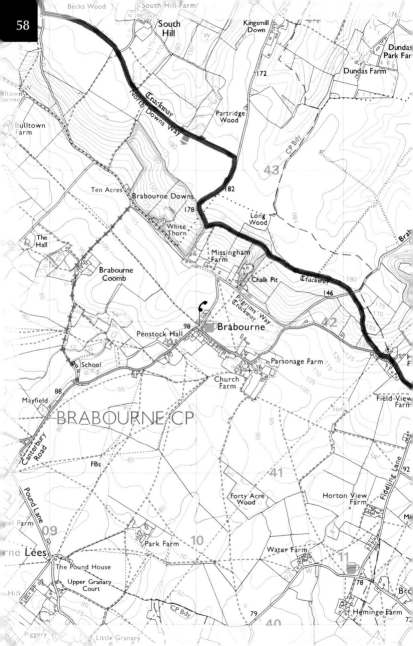

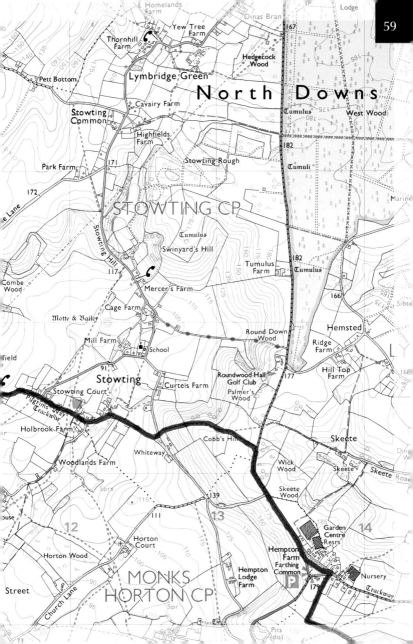

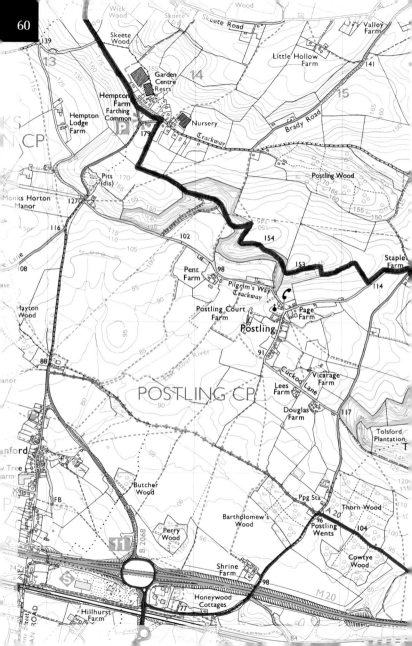

Wick Wood
Skeete Cott
Skeete Road
Wood
Valley Farm
139
13
Skeete Wood
Little Hollow Farm
141
14
Garden Centre Resrs
15
Brady Road
Hempton Farm
Hempton Lodge Farm
Farthing Common
Nursery
Trackway
Postling Wood
Pits (dis)
Monks Horton Manor
127
116
102
154
153
Staple Farm
108
Pent Farm
98
Pilgrim's Way Trackway
Page Farm
114
Hayton Wood
Postling Court Farm
Postling
91
88
Stour River
POSTLING CP
Cuckoo Lane
Vicarage Farm
Lees Farm
Douglas Farm
117
Tolsford Plantation
nford
Tree
FB
Butcher Wood
Ppg Sta
Thorn Wood
11
B 2068
Perry Wood
Bartholomew's Wood
A 20
Postling Wents
104
Cowtye Wood
Shrine Farm
98
Honeywood Cottages
77
M 20
Hillhurst Farm

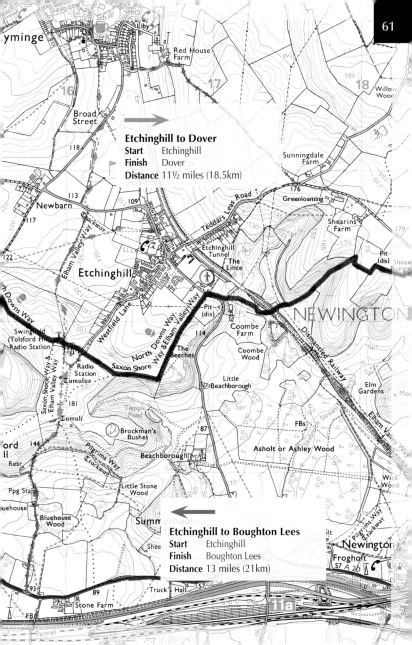

Etchinghill to Dover
Start Etchinghill
Finish Dover
Distance 11½ miles (18.5km)

Etchinghill to Boughton Lees
Start Etchinghill
Finish Boughton Lees
Distance 13 miles (21km)

Holmes Wood

Paddlesworth

Pit (dis)

Pit (dis)

Trackway

177

168

Sewage Works

Shearins Farm

179

180

Cole Farm

187

Sole Farm Resr

186 (192)

White Hall

Pit (dis)

Shearins Bungalow

BS

Home Farm

Parsonage Farm

Arpinge

173

Pits (disused)

164

Elving Farm

WINGTON CP

166

Lower Arpinge Farm

Gi

Elvingt

Arpinge Range

Pigeonhouse Wood

Upper Arpinge Farm

174

Grove Farm

131

Elm Gardens

Mound

175

Little Dane Farm

Upper Farm

Dismantled Railway

Spr

Spr

Elham Valley Way

Peene Quarry Country Park

Cheriton Hill

159

North Downs

Wood

98

Northcliffe

Danton Lane

Folkestone White Horse

Main Intake Substation

Wick Wood

Hill Lane

71

Peene

Pilgrims Way Trackway

Channel Tunnel Terminal

M20

Newington

Froglt House

Froholt

57 A 26

Pol Sta

Sch

Cheriton

12

Hotel

64 Sch

B 2064

FB

St Martin's Plain

66

Elham Valley Way

Underhill House

Sch

The Stadium

Risborough Barracks

Dibgate Camp

Casebourne Wood

32

Casebourne Farm

FB

63

Dibgate Farm

Scene

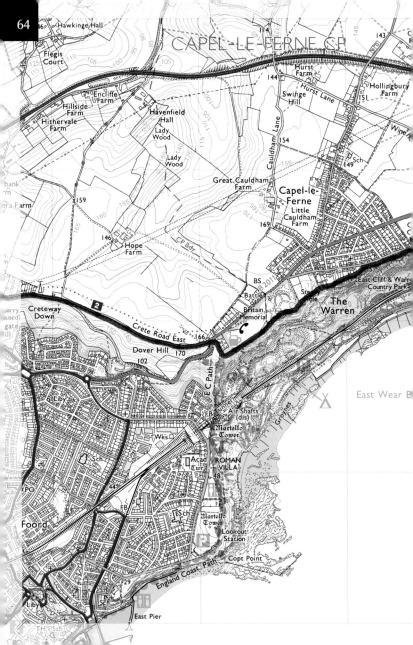

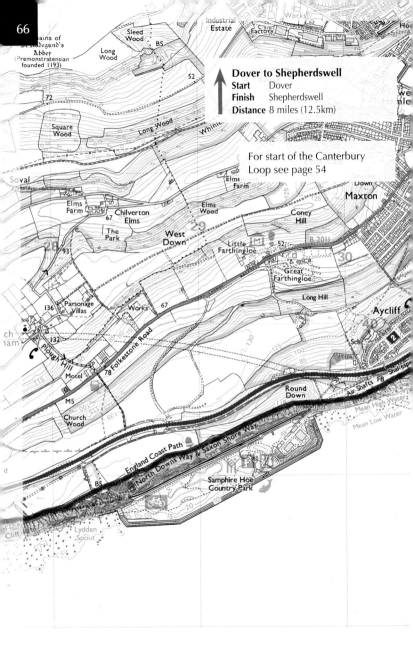

Dover to Shepherdswell

Start Dover
Finish Shepherdswell
Distance 8 miles (12.5km)

For start of the Canterbury
Loop see page 54

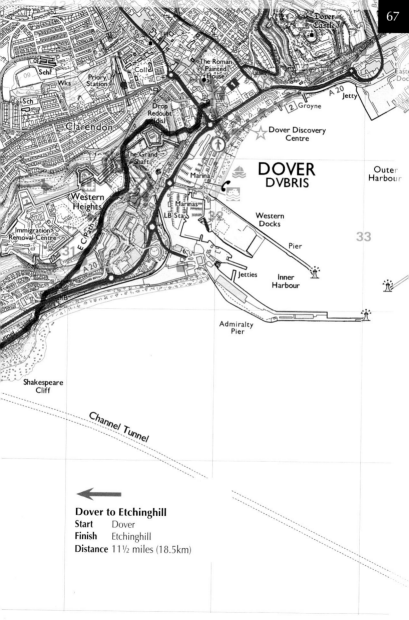

Dover to Etchinghill
Start Dover
Finish Etchinghill
Distance 11½ miles (18.5km)

Chilham

CHILHAM CP

Chilham Park

Mountain Street

Upper Ch... Dow...

Hurst Farm

Felborough Wood

Beech

Pole Wood

Great Hurst Wood

Danecourt Shaw

Dane Court

Dane Street

Ridge Wood

Cutlers Wood

Beeches

Yew

Playing Field

Soleshill Road

Howlett's Farm

Maggriyden

Pigeonhouse Wood

Young Manor Farm

Littlehurst Wood

Dolfinch Wood

Old Park Shaw

Park Wood

Cutlers

Yews

Chequers Farm

Denne Manor Farm

Denne

Cheyneys Farm

Manor La

Wytherling Court

Chalkrough

Beech

Stanners Wood

Beech

Old House Wood

Great Bower

Little Bower

Puddleduck Farm

Harts Farm

Flemings

Coppins Farm

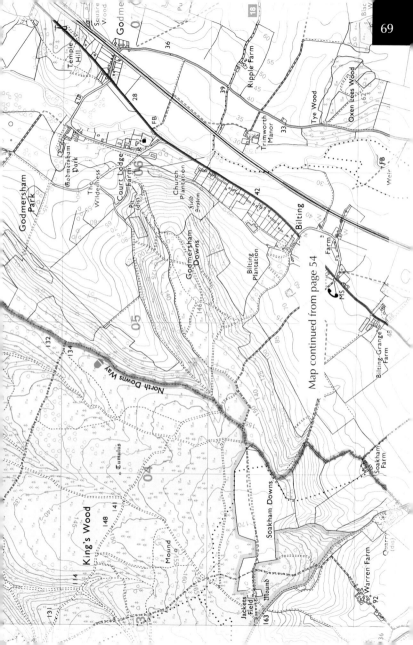

Map continued from page 54

Square Wood

Godme

Godmersham

Temple Hill

36

Ripple Farm

Tye Wood

Oxen Lees Wood

28

FB

Trimworth Manor

33

FB

Weir

Godmersham Park

The Wilderness

Court Lodge Farm

Pit (dis)

Church Plantation

Celtic Field System

42

Bilting

30

Bilting Farm

MS

Godmersham Downs

Bilting Plantation

Bilting Grange Farm

132

134

North Downs Way

King's Wood

114

131

148

141

145

Tumulus

Mound

Mound

Jackets Field

163

Soakham Downs

Soakham Farm

Warren Farm

Quarry

92

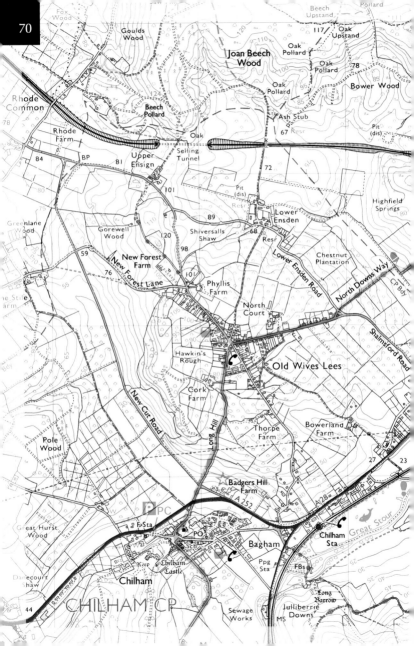

Primrose Hill
Petty
France
Pit
(dis)
Nature Reserve
77

Woodlands
Farm

Chartham
Hatch

83

Nickle
Wood

Hunstead
Wood

100

103

73

Howfield Lane

89

72

The Rough

37

Fright Wood
101

Hatch Lane

56

Langda
Wood

Nickle
Farm

Dunning
Shaw

Quarry
(dis)

Cemy

Ashford Rd

MS

22

24

FBs

Weir

18

Deanery
Farm

16

55

FB

Shalmsford
Bridge

18

Paper
Mill

Chartham

PO

21

Rentain
Farm

Court

23

Bobbin Lodge
Farm

Sch

Shalmsford
Street

rbury Road

Thruxted Lane

Stour Valley Walk

27

Mystole Road

Mystole Lane

54

ckelden Lane

28

73

21

School

Underdown

St A

Mystole
House

Mystole Park

41

CHARTHAM
CP

Thruxted

n

Sheep
Pens

Sprats
Wood

School

Perry Court
Farm

Upper Mystole
Park Farm

Blean Wood

Church Wood

New Road

New Road

HARBLEDOWN AND ROUGH COMMON CP

Stock Wood

Willows Wood

Homestall Wood

Harbledown Lodge

Motel

MS

Upper Harbledown

Stumps Farm

Staines Farm

FB

Denstead Lane

Poldhurst Farm

Bigbury

Sch

Denstead Farm

North Downs Way

Pit (dis)

Bigbury Farm

No Mans Orchard Nature Reserve

Bigbury Road

Bigbury Wood

Petty France

Pit (dis)

Howfield Wood

Tonford Manor Farm

Woodlands Farm

Howfield Wood Farm

Chartham Hatch

Howfield Lane

Howfield Farm

The Rough

Ppg Sta

Hotel

MS

Hatch

Langdane

Milton Manor

Sch

Park
Wood

Darwin Coll

Rutherford
Coll

73

69

36

Eliot
Coll

Moat

71

Keynes
Coll

University
of Kent

Sch

Kent
Coll

Sch

31

Sch

Hales
Place

A 290

Sch

PO

Rough
Common

Wr
Twr

College

St Stephen's

Neal's
Place

62

The
Grove

Cemy

Canterbury West
Station

St Dunstan's

Hospice

Sch

Schs

CATHEDRAL

Liby

Sch

MS 37

Harbledown

N D Way

Recn
Gd

18

A 290

Sch

PO

Golden
Hill

FB

Gorse Meadow
Farm

13

Acad

Sch

BSs

Bingley's
Island

Whitehall Meadows
Nature Reserve

Mon

FB

Stour Valley Walk

BS

9

FBs

9

Canterbury East
Station

Tonford
Manor

Riverside
Retail Park

P&R

Martyrs Field

37

Great Stour

Recn
Gd

A 28

18

Schs

FB

19

Sch

Wincheap Farm

22

Thanington

42

BS

Cockering
Farm

46

Pit
(dis)

38

Stuppington Lane

Pit

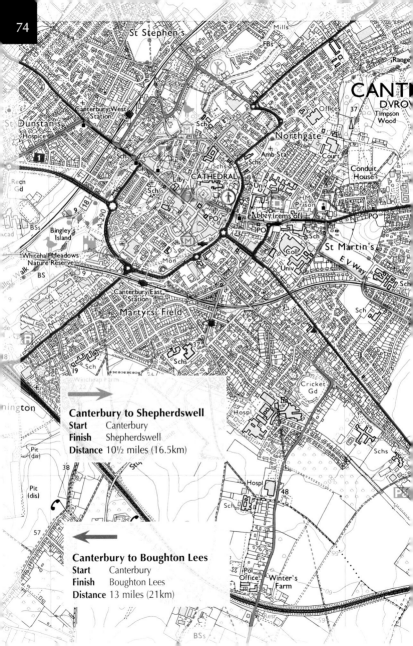

Canterbury to Shepherdswell
Start   Canterbury
Finish   Shepherdswell
Distance 10½ miles (16.5km)

Canterbury to Boughton Lees
Start   Canterbury
Finish   Boughton Lees
Distance 13 miles (21km)

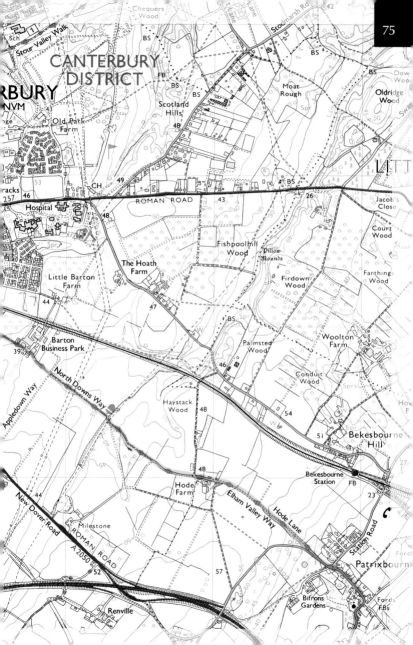

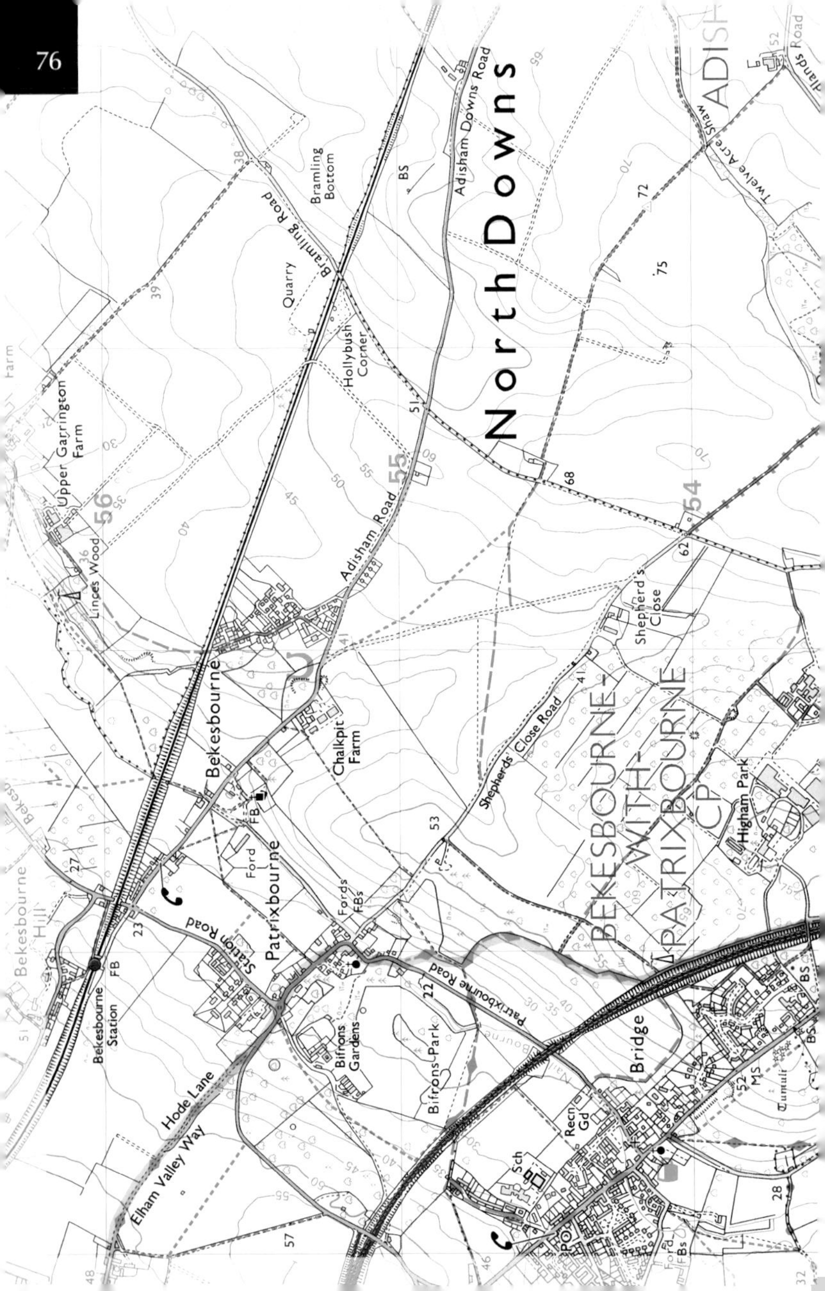

North Downs

ADISH

Adisham Downs Road

Twelve Acre Shaw

Bramling Road

Bramling Bottom

BS

Quarry

Hollybush Corner

Upper Garrington Farm

Linces Wood

56

Adisham Road

55

54

68

Shepherd's Close

BEKESBOURNE-WITH-PATRIXBOURNE CP

Bekesbourne

Chalkpit Farm

Shepherds Close Road

High31 Park

Highan Park

Ford

FB

Patrixbourne

Fords FBs

53

Bekesbourne Hill

27

Station Road

23

Bekesbourne Station

FB

Bifrons Gardens

Bifrons Park

Patrixbourne Road

22

Bridge

Tumulus

BS

BS

Hode Lane

Elham Valley Way

Recn Gd

Sch

28

FBs

57

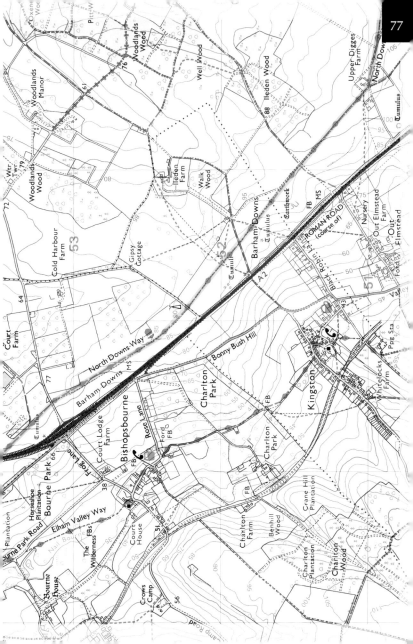

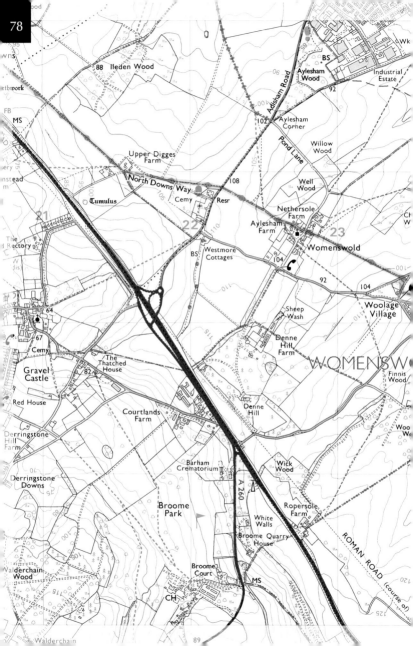

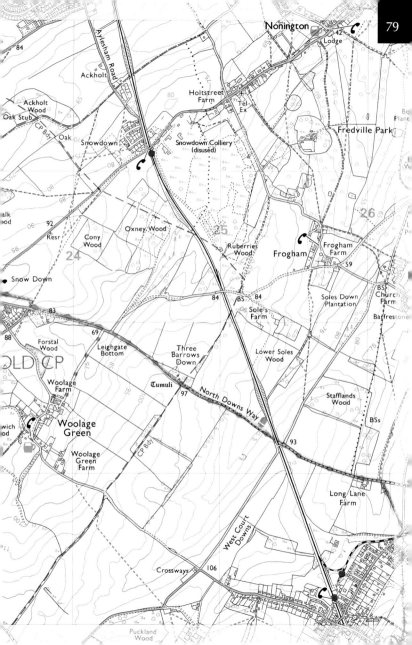

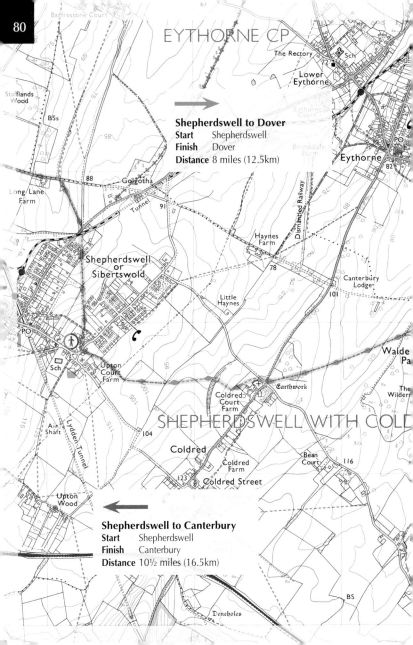

Shepherdswell to Dover
Start Shepherdswell
Finish Dover
Distance 8 miles (12.5km)

Shepherdswell to Canterbury
Start Shepherdswell
Finish Canterbury
Distance 10½ miles (16.5km)

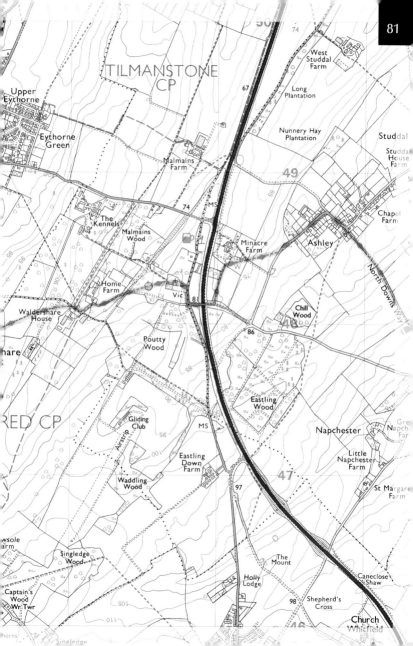

TILMANSTONE
CP

Upper
Eythorne

Eythorne
Green

Malmains
Farm

The
Kennels

Malmains
Wood

Home
Farm

Vic

Waldershare
House

Poutty
Wood

RED CP

Gliding
Club

Airstrip

Eastling
Down
Farm

Waddling
Wood

wsole
arm

Singledge
Wood

Captain's
Wood
Wr.Twr

horns

Singledge

West
Studdal
Farm

Long
Plantation

Nunnery Hay
Plantation

Studdal

Studdal
House
Farm

Chapel
Farm

Minacre
Farm

Ashley

North Downs Way

Chill
Wood

Eastling
Wood

Napchester

Gre
Napch
Far

Little
Napchester
Farm

St Margaret
Farm

The
Mount

Holly
Lodge

Caneclose
Shaw

Shepherd's
Cross

Church
Whitfield

MS

49

74

67

50

74

81

86

47

97

98

105

110

46

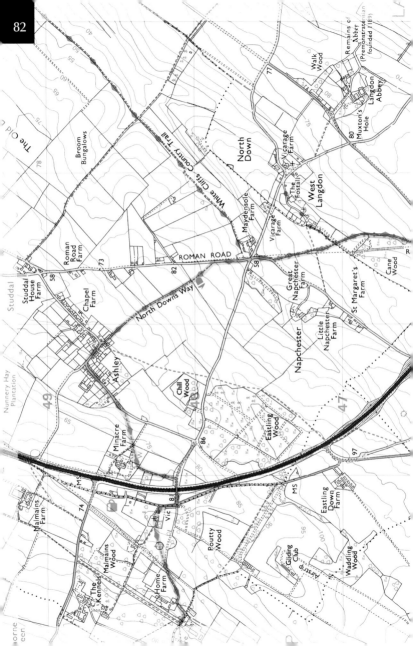

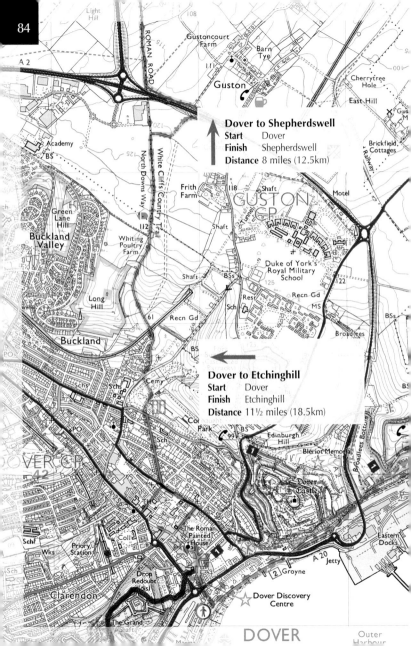

Dover to Shepherdswell

Start	Dover
Finish	Shepherdswell
Distance	8 miles (12.5km)

Dover to Etchinghill

Start	Dover
Finish	Etchinghill
Distance	11½ miles (18.5km)

LEGEND OF SYMBOLS
USED ON ORDNANCE SURVEY
1:25,000 (EXPLORER) MAPPING

ROADS AND PATHS   Not necessarily rights of way

M1 or A6(M)	Motorway
A 35	Dual carriageway
A30	Main road
B 3074	Secondary road
	Narrow road with passing places
	Road under construction
	Road generally more than 4 m wide
	Road generally less than 4 m wide
	Other road, drive or track, fenced and unfenced
»» »	Gradient: steeper than 20% (1 in 5); 14% (1 in 7) to 20% (1 in 5)
Ferry	Ferry; Ferry P – passenger only
....	Path

S Service Area   **7** Junction Number

S Service Area   **T1** Toll road junction

RAILWAYS

	Multiple track ⎱ standard
	Single track ⎰ gauge
—•—	Narrow gauge or Light rapid transit system (LRTS) and station
	Road over; road under; level crossing
	Cutting; tunnel; embankment
—●—	Station, open to passengers; siding

PUBLIC RIGHTS OF WAY

- - - - - - -	Footpath
— — — —	Bridleway
+ + + + +	Byway open to all traffic
⊥ ⊥ ⊥ ⊥	Restricted byway

The representation on this map of any other road, track or path is no evidence of the existence of a right of way

ARCHAEOLOGICAL AND HISTORICAL INFORMATION

✛	Site of antiquity	VILLA	Roman	⋰ ▦	Visible earthwork
⚔ 1066	Site of battle (with date)	Castle	Non-Roman		

Information provided by English Heritage for England and the Royal Commissions on the Ancient and Historical Monuments for Scotland and Wales

OTHER PUBLIC ACCESS

• • •	Other routes with public access

The exact nature of the rights on these routes and the existence of any restrictions may be checked with the local highway authority. Alignments are based on the best information available

◆ ◆ ◆	Recreational route
◆ ◆ ◆	🚶 National Trail ⟨🏃⟩ Long Distance Route
------------	Permissive footpath
– – – – –	Permissive bridleway

Footpaths and bridleways along which landowners have permitted public use but which are not rights of way. The agreement may be withdrawn

• • •	Traffic-free cycle route
1 **1**	National cycle network route number – traffic free; on road

ACCESS LAND

 Firing and test ranges in the area. Danger! Observe warning notices

 Access permitted within managed controls, for example, local byelaws. Visit **www.access.mod.uk** for information

England and Wales

 Access land boundary and tint

Access land in wooded area

 Access information point

Portrayal of access land on this map is intended as a guide to land which is normally available for access on foot, for example access land created under the Countryside and Rights of Way Act 2000, and land managed by the National Trust, Forestry Commission and Woodland Trust. Access for other activities may also exist. Some restrictions will apply; some land will be excluded from open access rights. The depiction of rights of access does not imply or express any warranty as to its accuracy or completeness. Observe local signs and follow the Countryside Code.
Visit **www.countrysideaccess.gov.uk** for up-to-date information

BOUNDARIES

— + — +	National
— · — · —	County (England)
— — — —	Unitary Authority (UA), Metropolitan District (Met Dist), London Borough (LB) or District
	(Scotland & Wales are solely Unitary Authorities)
· · · · · · · · · · ·	Civil Parish (CP) (England) or Community (C) (Wales)
▬▬▬ ▬▬▬	National Park boundary

VEGETATION

Limits of vegetation are defined by positioning of symbols

⫲ ⫲	Coniferous trees
⚬ᵒ ⚬ᵒ	Non-coniferous trees
₌ₐ ₌ₐ	Coppice
⚬ ⚬ ⚬ ⚬	Orchard
₀ₓ ₀ₓ	Scrub
⁖	Bracken, heath or rough grassland
⁓	Marsh, reeds or saltings

HEIGHTS AND NATURAL FEATURES

52 ·	Ground survey height
284 ·	Air survey height

Surface heights are to the nearest metre above mean sea level. Where two heights are shown, the first height is to the base of the triangulation pillar and the second (in brackets) to the highest natural point of the hill

HEIGHTS AND NATURAL FEATURES

52 ·   Ground survey height
284 ·   Air survey height

Surface heights are to the nearest metre above mean sea level. Where two heights are shown, the first height is to the base of the triangulation pillar and the second (in brackets) to the highest natural point of the hill

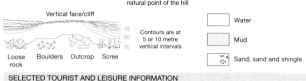

Vertical face/cliff

Loose rock   Boulders   Outcrop   Scree

75
60   Contours are at
50   5 or 10 metre
      vertical intervals

☐ Water

☐ Mud

☐ Sand; sand and shingle

SELECTED TOURIST AND LEISURE INFORMATION

🏛	Building of historic interest	🐦	Nature reserve
⚙	Cadw	🏵	National Trust
HC	Heritage centre	☆	Other tourist feature
🏕	Camp site	P	Parking
🚐	Caravan site	P&R	Park and ride, all year
🚐🏕	Camping and caravan site	P&R	Park and ride, seasonal
🏰	Castle / fort	✕	Picnic site
✝	Cathedral / Abbey	🚂	Preserved railway
⚒	Craft centre	PC	Public Convenience
🎪	Country park	🍺	Public house/s
🚲	Cycle trail	🏃	Recreation / leisure / sports centre
🚵	Mountain bike trail	🏛	Roman site (Hadrian's Wall only)
🚲	Cycle hire	⚓	Slipway
⊞	English Heritage	📞	Telephone, emergency
🎣	Fishing	📞	Telephone, public
🌲	Forestry Commission Visitor centre	📞	Telephone, roadside assistance
❀	Garden / arboretum	🎡	Theme / pleasure park
🚩	Golf course or links	🔆	Viewpoint
📕	Historic Scotland	Ⓥ	Visitor centre
𝒊	Information centre, all year	❗	Walks / trails
𝒊	Information centre, seasonal	◈	World Heritage site / area
⋃	Horse riding	⛵	Water activites
🏛	Museum	⛵	Boat trips
🐾	National Park Visitor Centre (park logo) e.g. Yorkshire Dales	⛴	Boat hire

(For complete legend and symbols, see any OS Explorer map).

THE NORTH DOWNS WAY

This map booklet accompanies Kev Reynolds' guidebook to walking the North Downs Way National Trail between Farnham and Dover. The guidebook features annotated 1:50,000 mapping alongside detailed step-by-step route descriptions and extensive information about this popular bridleway.

WALKING THE
NORTH DOWNS WAY

NATIONAL TRAIL
From Farnham to Dover

Kev Reynolds

INCLUDES
1:25,000
ROUTE MAP
BOOKLET

CICERONE

Carved from a storm-damaged tree, this piece of sculpture stands above the trail near the Kent/Surrey border